Sustainable Cities
Inspirational Case Studies

Sustainable Cities
Inspirational Case Studies

Edited by Simon Mills

LONDON AND NEW YORK

First published 2015 by Greenleaf Publishing Limited

Published 2017 by Routledge
2 Park Square, Milton Park, Abingdon, Oxon OX14 4RN
711 Third Avenue, New York, NY 10017, USA

Routledge is an imprint of the Taylor & Francis Group, an informa business

Copyright © 2015 Taylor & Francis

All rights reserved. No part of this book may be reprinted or reproduced or utilised in any form or by any electronic, mechanical, or other means, now known or hereafter invented, including photocopying and recording, or in any information storage or retrieval system, without permission in writing from the publishers.

Notice:
Product or corporate names may be trademarks or registered trademarks, and are used only for identification and explanation without intent to infringe.

British Library Cataloguing in Publication Data:
    A catalogue record for this book is available from the British Library.

ISBN-13: 978-1-78353-1-653 [pbk]
ISBN-13: 978-1-78353-196-7 [hbk]

Contents

Foreword..vii
    The Right Honourable The Lord Mayor of the City of London,
    Alderman Fiona Woolf CBE

Introduction..1
    Simon Mills MSc MPA, Head of Sustainable Development
    for the City of London

About the Sustainable City Awards..3

Sustainable City Award Winners...5

About the City of London..10

GrowUp Urban Farms......................................12
Award: Entrepreneurship (commercial)

Project Dirt...21
Award: Entrepreneurship (commercial)

Rosh Engineering.......................................31
Award: Entrepreneurship (commercial)

PleaseCycle (now Yomp) 40
Award: Entrepreneurship (social)

Core Arts 51
Award: Greening the Third Sector

Abundance 60
Award: Sustainable Finance

Co-oproduct CIC 67
Award: Responsible Waste Management & Social Entrepreneurship

Nampak Plastics 75
Award: Responsible Waste Management

Castle Climbing Centre 83
Award: Responsible Waste Management/Sustainable Food

United House, NHP Leisure Developments and Mitsubishi Electric (joint award) 93
Award: Sustainable Building

WestTrans Partnership 112
Award: Sustainable Travel and Transport

Foreword

The Right Honourable The Lord Mayor of the City of London, Alderman Fiona Woolf CBE

The core theme of my tenure as Lord Mayor of London has been Tomorrow's City – the energy to transform lives. Nowhere is the essence of this theme better brought to life than in the Sustainable Cities awards.

Those represented in this collection, kindly brought to you by Greenleaf Publishing, include community groups, the public sector, small business, and multinationals. The one thing that binds all of these groups together is sustainability.

Sustainable organizations are successful organizations. Sustainability brings clear benefits by reducing risk, opening up new markets, and improving staff morale. Sustainability is not an optional extra, to be discarded when the chill winds of the recession begin to blow. It is an essential shield which can protect businesses, and give them a springboard for rapid growth as the economy begins to thaw. It is the rocket fuel that will drive growth, jobs and quality of life for all.

I am delighted that the City of London and our partners have been able to recognize the outstanding qualities of our winners, and offer them my heartfelt congratulations on their success.

Fiona Woolf

Introduction

Simon Mills MSc MPA
Head of Sustainable Development for the City of London

I must admit that when I established the Sustainable City Awards back in 2000, I had no idea they would grow to become the institution they are today.

According to the RSA the average life expectancy of an awards scheme is three years, which is why, to qualify for RSA accreditation, awards have to demonstrate longevity as well as stringent standards of quality and transparency.

Personally I put the success of the Sustainable City Awards down to three things:

- Firstly the efforts of our army of partner organizations (22 and counting) who work tirelessly to promote the awards, and sift and separate the hundreds of entries we receive for the awards every year.
- Secondly the draw of the City of London – the fact that the world's leading international business centre hosts these awards, underscores the importance of sustainable business practice – as a

driver of growth, a driver of efficiency and a driver of innovation.

- Finally, and most importantly, the quality of the applications – office recycling schemes and bike racks are no longer seen as exceptions, they are, to borrow a phrase from the Lord Mayor, "the new normal". Today's Sustainable City Awards are a celebration of excellence, a salutation of the exceptional, not as novelty, but as the standard for tomorrow's companies.

Over the past fourteen years it has been my pleasure and my privilege to hear about the journeys of some of the UK's most forward-thinking and successful firms. I am delighted that Greenleaf Publishing have enabled us to share some of these stories with you.

About the Sustainable City Awards

The Sustainable City Awards were established in 2001 by the City of London Corporation to recognize and reward organizations that have demonstrated excellence in sustainable development. Examples of this have included logistics companies that are reducing congestion and air pollution, organizations that are helping people with visual impairments into employment, ethical pensions funds, and plastics manufacturers with state-of-the-art recycling programmes.

The awards run annually, and are launched in September with the awards ceremony hosted at Mansion House the following March. Due to extensive media coverage in print and broadcast media, the Awards are now considered the UK's foremost sustainable development awards scheme.

The awards, which do not charge for entry or for attendance at the Mansion House awards ceremony, attract an average of 250 entries from organizations across the UK ranging from household names to community groups. The Sustainable City Awards are supported by 22 partners, and are given across 12 categories, which between them represent the three pillars of sustainable development: the economy, society and the environment. The partners supporting each category set up judging panels, which choose a winner, a highly commended entry and three shortlisted organizations. The winner and the highly commended entry for each category are put forward for consideration for two further awards:

- The business entries are considered for the Sir Alan Parker Award
- All of the winning and highly commended entries are considered for the Sustainable City Trophy

Previous winners of the Sustainable City Trophy have included charities, community groups, small family-run businesses and multinational companies. The Awards have been selected as a national feeder scheme for the European Business Awards, by the Royal Society for the Arts.

For more information, see www.cityoflondon.gov.uk/services/environment-and-planning/sustainability/sustainable-city-awards.

Sustainable City Award Winners

(Italics denotes cases included within this collection.)

Sustainable Finance Category
(supported by the UK Sustainable Investment and Finance Association)
- *Abundance Generation *winner**
- Resonance – Real Lettings Property Fund *highly commended*
- The Ecology Building Society
- Impax Investment Management
- Schroders Investment Management

Sustainable Travel and Transport
(supported by the Campaign for Better Transport).
- GetMoreBikes *winner*
- *WestTrans Partnership *highly commended**
- Bradford Council for WYLES
- CC Cycles
- E-car club Ltd

Responsible Waste Management
(supported by the Clean City Awards)
- Zoological Society of London *winner*
- *Nampak Plastics Europe Ltd *highly commended**
- *The Castle Climbing Centre*
- Cavendish Conference Centre
- *Co-oproduct CIC*

Resource Conservation
(supported by The Worshipful Company of Launderers and The Worshipful Company of Water Conservators)
- Zoological Society of London *winner*
- Redbridge Lakes *highly commended*
- The Cavendish Conference Centre

Sustainable Building
(supported by the Worshipful Company of Chartered Surveyors and The Chartered Institute of Building)
- *United House and NHP Leisure Developments for their Kingston Heights development *winner**
- The South West Energy Centre *highly commended*
- Belfast Metropolitan College for their e3 Centre
- Nottingham City Homes for their "Secure Warm Modern" programme
- Skanska for Brent Civic Centre

Sustainable Food
(supported by the Chartered Institute of Environmental Health)
- *The Castle Climbing Centre *winner**
- Vacherin Ltd *highly commended*
- The Clink Charity
- Shropshire Energy (UK) Ltd
- Wahaca Restaurants

Entrepreneurship (Social)
(supported by the Worshipful Company of Environmental Cleaners, the London Sustainability Exchange and The Energy Saving Trust)
- *Please Cycle *winner**
- GetMore *highly commended*
- Co-oproduct CIC
- London Youth
- Nottingham City Homes
- Redbridge Lakes

Entrepreneurship (Social)
(supported by the Worshipful Company of Environmental Cleaners, the London Sustainability Exchange and the Energy Saving Trust)
- Carbon Voyage *winner*
- *Rosh Engineering Ltd *highly commended**
- E-car club Ltd
- Project Dirt Ltd
- GrowUp Urban Farms Ltd

Farsight Award
(supported by Gresham College and the Zyen Group Ltd)

Entries to the Farsight Award are drawn from contributors to The London Accord project, the world's largest collaborative research programme on sustainable finance.
- Lloyds of London *winner*
- Bank of America Merrill Lynch *highly commended*
- Kepler Cheuvreux *highly commended*
- HSBC
- Sustainalytics

Greening the Third Sector

(supported by the Worshipful Company of Patten Makers and the City Bridge Trust)

- Poplar HARCA *winner*
- Get More *highly commended*
- London Youth *highly commended*
- *Core Arts*
- New Horizon Youth Centre

Air Quality

(supported by King's College London)

- Nomura International plc *winner*
- Bradford City Council *highly commended*
- GetMoreBikes *highly commended*
- Lend Lease
- ClientEarth

Tackling Climate Change

(supported by the Ecological Sequestration Trust and the Institute of Sustainability)

- Shropshire Energy (UK) Ltd *winner*
- *The Castle Climbing Centre *highly commended**
- Climate Solutions Fund
- *United House and NHP Leisure Developments*

Sustainable Fashion

(supported by the British Fashion Council)

- Thrifty Couture *winner*
- The Good Wardrobe (highly commended)
- Rentez Vous
- Tammam

Winner of the 2014 Sustainable City Trophy:
Rosh Engineering

About the City of London

The City Corporation has a special role and wide remit that goes beyond that of an ordinary local authority. It looks after the City of London on behalf of all who live, work and visit here and has three primary functions:

- It supports and promotes the City as the world leader in international finance and business services.
- It provides modern, efficient and high-quality local services and policing within the Square Mile for residents, workers and visitors.
- It provides valued services to London and the nation as a whole, including its role as one of the most significant arts sponsors in the UK and its support for economic regeneration in the surrounding boroughs.

Many of these services are funded from its own resources at no cost to the public and benefit London and the nation. Its valued services include:

- The Barbican Centre and the Guildhall School of Music & Drama
- The Guildhall Library and Art Gallery and London Metropolitan Archives
- A range of education provision including three City Academies
- The maintenance of five Thames bridges (including Tower Bridge and the Millennium Bridge)
- Management of the Central Criminal Court at Old Bailey
- Management of almost 11,000 acres of some of London's best-loved open spaces including Hampstead Heath and Epping Forest
- Management of three wholesale food markets (Billingsgate, Smithfield and New Spitalfields)
- It also provide London's Port Health Authority and run the Animal Reception Centre at Heathrow.

It works in partnership with neighbouring boroughs on the regeneration of surrounding areas and its charity, the City Bridge Trust, donates more than £15m to charity annually.

The City of London views sustainability as a critical component of resilience and fundamental to the competitiveness of London and the nation.

GrowUp Urban Farms

www.growup.org.uk

Award: Entrepreneurship (commercial)

The Mission

GrowUp Urban Farms grows sustainable and healthy salads, herbs and fish in cities using aquaponics and vertical growing systems. Aquaponics is a combination of two well established farming practices – aquaculture (farming fish) and hydroponics (growing plants in a nutrient solution instead of soil). We take the waste water from a fish farm, and pump it through our hydroponic growing beds where our salad plants absorb the waste nutrients from the water, clean the water for the fish, and the whole system continually recirculates.

Our mission is to feed people in cities in a positive way for the community and for the environment, today and in the future. We do this through creating employment and lowering the environmental impact of agriculture.

We see what we do as sitting at the heart of the conversation around Sustainable Cities – by reducing the environmental impact of how we feed people in cities we can start to adapt our cities in response to climate change and mitigate against further climate change impact in agriculture. Cities that have a more sustainable way of sourcing and producing food create less harm to the environment, where problems associated with traditional farming methods include leaching of fertilizers and pesticides, disruption to ecosystems through habitat loss and a high water requirement.

The Challenge

Growing food in cities and making that process transparent for people is a key part of the challenge of reconnecting people with the story of where their food comes from and what it takes to produce it.

The challenge of sustainable food production that can contribute to local food security is one that many cities face. Traditional agriculture requires transportation of the produce to the city, and this travel time reduces the freshness of produce and can lead to higher levels of waste. Urban production reduces transportation distances and therefore has the potential to reduce embodied carbon in food.

Traditional farming relies on fertilizers and pesticides that can have detrimental effects on the surrounding area. Through leaching into water sources, the ecosystem structure can be altered and damaged. Future food production needs to minimize its impact on the environment, reduce reliance on chemical-based fertilizers and pesticides and in addition, reduce the amount of water required for food production.

Feeding people in cities needs to be readdressed to take into account the potential of urban farming – not as a replacement for traditional agriculture, but as one part of the solution of creating cities that are more self-sufficient and more sustainable in their use and reuse of resources.

Developing Sustainable Solutions

Image 1: The GrowUp Box

In 2013 we built our prototype farm – The GrowUp Box. Designed to maximize the yield from a restricted growing space, the GrowUp Box is a demonstration farm that incorporates both aquaponics and vertical growing systems in one space. Made from a recycled shipping container with a greenhouse on top, the Box houses an aquaponics system capable of holding up to 150 fish and 450 salads at any one time (see Image 1). The greenhouse allows for year-round growing, with crops changed to adapt to seasonal conditions. Our use of aquaponic technology addresses the challenge of reducing water supply and providing a natural way to fertilize the plants. The soilless nature of the system minimizes water loss that is usually associated with soil-based growing, where water is lost through evaporation and absorption into the ground. The cycling of water between the fish and the plants means the nutrients are absorbed and replaced, decreasing the need for more water and removing the need for additional fertilizers (see Image 2).

Our vertical growing techniques also means that the growing density is higher than traditional growing methods. The greenhouse holds 40 vertical growing columns each capable of holding between 10 and 15 plants. The water is pumped through the internal structure of the columns while the plants grow on the external surface of the columns.

The GrowUp Box was built following a successful crowdfunding campaign that raised over £16,500 on Kickstarter from more than 300 supporters, creating a support base for the project and indicating a growing interest in sustainable food production around the world.

The GrowUp Box is designed to be used in any unused urban space. Cities have the potential to turn unused space into productive growing spaces – this includes the rooftops of buildings, unused land and disused car parks.

SUSTAINABLE CITIES

Image 2: Aquaponic system

Not only does this activate unused space, it also compares favourably to the impact that traditional farming can have when disrupting habitats and ecosystems in rural areas. The shipping container is a highly visible way of presenting aquaponics, and also creates a secure environment for the system making it suitable for public spaces and interaction.

The Box was also designed to give people the opportunity to see aquaponics in action and learn about sustainable urban food production. We've held workshops and open days at the GrowUp Box to engage the local community about aquaponics and sustainability. Rather than focusing on "grow your own", our approach educates people on what it takes to produce food, allowing them to make more informed, and hopefully healthier and more sustainable choices about the food they buy and eat.

The Box was open to the public on weekends (and Fridays throughout the school holidays) over the summer of 2013. The aim of this was to engage with the local community and discuss the pros and cons of the current food system, how what we do is different, what place we have in the food system and how we plan to get there. When the Box first opened to the public it was as part of the Chelsea Fringe Festival. We continued to receive a fair amount of press and promotion around our work, which we encouraged as this often led to more visitors coming to see us. We were featured in articles in publications including Time out, The BBC, Guardian, Inhabitat and Sustain Magazine. These can all be found through our Pinterest board: www.pinterest.com/growupbox/growup-in-the-press.

The produce grown in the GrowUp Box is sold to local restaurants. This allowed us to test the market for our produce, and gain valuable insight into the requirements of local independent restaurants – our target market for sustainably produced salads, herbs and fish.

Experiences

The GrowUp Box is a proof of concept for GrowUp Urban Farms and created the springboard from which we've been able to propose a viable model for scaling our business to maximize our social and environmental impact. There are two key areas in which we've learned lessons around the operation of the Box as a point of public engagement and education and are now putting that knowledge to use:

Design

The GrowUp Box was a prototype system, designed to maximize the productive yield from a small urban space and give us the opportunity to engage with potential customers and the local community. Over the first year of operations, we worked closely with a number of volunteers who helped with the operations of the box to redesign and refit the growing system. We've also continued to work with an architectural designer to look at what modifications would need to be made to the overall design to make it appropriate for sale as a stand-alone unit. This included technical changes to increase the efficiency of the system and to increase the ease of working in the greenhouse as well as alterations to ensure the Box met Building Regulations for school buildings. This has resulted in a "Box

2.0" design which we are now working on developing as an independent business proposition.

Volunteers/training

We continue to receive a significant number of requests from people who are interested in volunteering at the Box or who would like to learn more about aquaponics. This suggests that there is a gap in the market for courses around aquaponics in urban areas and something that we will explore in the future. In terms of bringing on volunteers, we want to make sure we can do this in a structured and mutually beneficial way. This year we're working with Urban Food Routes who are helping us design a volunteering programme to put in place at the Box.

The Future

In late 2014, GrowUp will build London's first commercial aquaponic urban farm, demonstrating the viability of high density aquaponic production in urban and peri-urban areas. With production planned to start in early 2015, this farm will generate employment opportunities for local young people with a poor record of educational attainment, and will be capable of producing around 20,000 kg of salad and 5,000 kg of fish each year.

In 2015 we also hope to start marketing the GrowUp Box as a product available for schools and universities to use as an educational tool to explore sustainable and local food production.

The GrowUp Box continues to operate, selling produce to local restaurants around Stratford in East London and offering workshops and open events for people to learn about aquaponics and urban farming.

Authors

Prior to forming GrowUp Urban Farms, **Kate Hofman** (Co-founder) worked as a management consultant for IBM. Whilst on a sabbatical year at Imperial College London, she began investigating how aquaponics could work as a sustainable way of commercially growing food for London. Her overriding philosophy is that innovation and sustainability are at the core of the best businesses.

Tom Webster (Co-founder)'s commitment to sustainable food production has always underpinned his professional life. During his MSc, he looked at the benefits and potential supplementary uses of green roofs in the city. Working as a sustainability consultant he continued to investigate the potential for rooftop farming in London. This work, combined with his background in biology, led Tom to found GrowUp Urban Farms in 2013 with Kate.

info@growup.org.uk

PROJECTDIRT
CONNECTING COMMUNITIES FOR GOOD

Project Dirt
www.projectdirt.com

Award: Entrepreneurship (commercial)

The Mission

Project Dirt is a social networking platform that links up over 2,000 community and environmental projects across the UK. Our core mission is to connect, promote and resource the amazing projects that are happening at a grassroots level. To achieve better resourcing of community projects, we work with companies, local authorities and third sector organizations who can utilize Project Dirt to distribute resources like volunteers, funding, equipment and event space to community projects.

We are passionate about the creation of sustainable cities. Cities are highly attractive places for people to live: the majority of the world's population already lives in cities,[1] and in a few decades cities could be home to as much as two-thirds of the world's population. Whilst environmental problems, such as air pollution, drainage

---

[1] United Nations (2014) 'World Urbanization Prospects' (New York: United Nations; http://esa.un.org/unpd/wup/Highlights/WUP2014-Highlights.pdf, accessed on 22 September 2014).

and sanitation, can be particularly apparent and pressing with densely populated living arrangements, cities can offer huge sustainability advantages linked to lower land consumption and shorter travelling distances. However, what we are most passionate about is the fact that cities are places where people and businesses aggregate and, as a consequence, ideas for change abound and exciting projects emerge.

The Challenge

Having been engaged in urban community projects in South London for some time Project Dirt's founders, Nick Gardner and Mark Shearer, saw a significant lack of connection between urban community groups – despite a massive increase in such grassroots activity in recent years. There was no means of linking these initiatives up with each other, and nowhere to systematically share best practice and resources. This gave rise to three challenges:

1. **Lack of learning.** Projects had to constantly reinvent the wheel, without being able to benefit from the learning that had taken part in other community projects, even where that happened only a few miles away.
2. **Lack of engagement.** There used to be a large gap in terms of mass engagement of willing people giving their time, skills and expertise for local community-based projects to collectively make a significant difference. This happened in isolated pockets, but we saw significant potential for scale.

3. **Inefficient resource distribution.** There has been a particular disconnect between those that are in acute need of resources – grassroots projects – and those that are capable of giving, such as businesses. With limited time and resources at hand fundraising, for example, can be a real challenge for many community projects.

An engaging social network was needed to link up these urban community projects, to promote their activities to a wider public and to resource their initiatives more efficiently – in order to join the dots and achieve bigger change in the cities that we live in.

Developing Sustainable Solutions

Increasingly companies and local authorities are working on the "smart cities" agenda, to make intelligent use of the vast wealth of data that now exists to enable cities to run more efficiently. Whilst this agenda is progressing at pace, it is largely focused on technical and mechanical data … and the "people" element is getting left behind.

We believe that it is people – their passions, and their skills – that are the driving power behind what makes cities really work. A truly sustainable city engages its citizens in making priority changes to the urban landscape and lifestyle.

Bringing passionate people together to make change happen at a local level is what we wanted to do. Social media offered the opportunity to tap into the fantastic human resource that exists, and utilize them to their best effect to make a truly "sustainable" city.

With the aim of tackling the challenges outlined in the section above, Project Dirt was created in South London in 2008. The idea behind Project Dirt is to use social media for a purpose: to connect, promote and resource passionate people and their projects.

Originally built on a Ning platform, Project Dirt's founders soon realized that more complex networking capabilities were needed and launched their bespoke website in late 2012. This enabled the site to grow to a national scale, whilst still retaining a local focus for individual users and visitors to the site.

In the same year Project Dirt started to work with London-based businesses, local authorities and third-sector organizations on a commercial level, always with the keen aim to help local community projects receive more resources more easily. The team developed a business model which allows clients to utilize Project Dirt to distribute resources like volunteers, funding, equipment and event space to community projects. Project Dirt enables them to do this far more effectively, achieving greater credibility and attracting much wider public visibility in the process.

To date, we have distributed over £150,000 of new funds into community projects, helped to place hundreds of volunteers – both from the general public, and from our corporate partners, and have had over 12,000 events added to our event listings directory.

One example of a successful campaign that we are supporting in the capital is the Mayor of London's Pocket Parks programme, through which 100 new small parks are being created all across the City.[2] Pocket Parks are green oases through which Londoners can seek "relief from the hustle and bustle of the city".[3] They are not only key for people's well-being; Pocket Parks are also of immense importance for the local climate and biodiversity, and are thus key factors for urban sustainability. Project Dirt allows project leads, volunteers and the public to exchange information about best practice examples and events, as well as to celebrate their success stories with local people and the wider public. After 18 months an impressive resource has developed that tells the story of dozens of projects, organizations and local authorities transforming places they care about.

With international law firm Olswang we launched a further successful campaign, focused around the company's own "Green Seed Fund".[4] The Fund is an innovative way to make carbon neutrality more meaningful to the local community, through funding local urban environmental projects. Partnering with Project Dirt enabled Olswang to have the maximum impact with its resources and to reach out to a much wider community. While the company received 5 applications for the Green Seed Fund in 2013, prior to Project Dirt's involvement, in 2014 over 100 creative and inspiring community projects applied. This has allowed to Olswang to successfully meet the objectives

---

2   See www.projectdirt.com/pocketparks.
3   Greater London Authority (2014) "Pocket Parks Programme" (London: Greater London Authority; https://www.london.gov.uk/priorities/environment/greening-london/improving-londons-parks-green-spaces/pocket-parks, accessed on 22 September 2014).
4   See www.projectdirt.com/olswang.

behind the Green Seed Fund – to have a positive environmental impact in the areas local to their offices and to strengthen the firm's connection with its local community and staff. Project Dirt and Olswang will continue to work together through its own "cluster page" hosted on Project Dirt, where all the winning Green Seed Fund projects are starting to populate their pages with images and blog entries with updates on how they are putting their funding to good use.

Figure 1: Blog post from Share Community, one of Olswang's Green Seed Fund Grantees[5]

Experiences

It's working. An external evaluation undertaken in 2013 found that more than two-thirds of Project Dirt users have

---

5   See www.projectdirt.com/olswang.

been actively involved with projects on our site, and 40% of project leads had contributed to projects other than their own. The user survey suggested that Project Dirt is having significant influence in terms of deepening participation, through helping to ensure that the appropriate motivations, triggers, resources and opportunities for participation are in place. Two in three project leads have found volunteers through Project Dirt, .

Figure 2: Using Project Dirt to get involved[6]

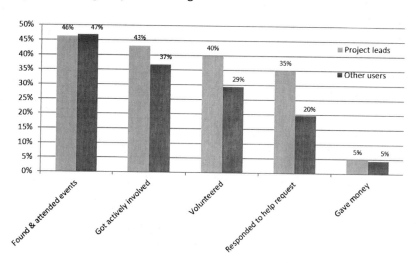

However, establishing and embedding a new kind of community website has not been without its challenges. Over the past few years, we have learned many lessons which we're more than happy to share!

Firstly, it's important not to "reinvent the wheel". Whilst we say this all the time to people wanting to set up their

---

[6] Pratt, J.; Matthews, S.; Lipscomb, L.; Jeeps, R. (2013) *An Evaluation of Project Dirt* (Canterbury, UK: Emergent Research & Consulting).

own community projects, we also practise what we preach for our own website. When we set Project Dirt up, there was quite simply nothing out there doing what we do. However, no website is built from scratch, and so we used existing (free) tools in the outset, and only set about designing our own when we outgrew these. We could have added plenty of other functions for our groups, such as "crowdfunding" capabilities, but these are done well by other organizations and so we are seeking to establish strategic partnerships to extend our site's functionality.

Secondly, we have learned to be inclusive. Our online community is our main strength, and so we have asked them to help us design our website at key stages of the process, and have kept them informed every step of the way. This kind of inclusive design has really helped us to galvanize and strengthen the feeling of shared ownership over our site! We probably could have made better use of our community ambassadors programme, which we're hoping to reinstate shortly.

Thirdly, perseverance. The road ahead for a startup with new ideas to improve urban sustainability is rarely straightforward. Even when doing things which most other people have told us is fantastic, we have had naysayers and received negative vibes from certain individuals along the way. And there have certainly been roadblocks – funders pulling out at the last minute; promises being broken and dead-ends aplenty. Belief in the longer-term goal has kept us going through the difficult times.

The Future

Looking to the future, our plans are to really grow Project Dirt beyond its roots in London, and embed further into the key cities around the country. This base-rock of activity will allow us to explore more carefully how we can take the "easy" networking opportunities provided by cities, and adapt the model to work well in smaller towns, villages and rural areas. Beyond that, in a year or two, we should be in a position to take our model beyond the UK.

We are also poised to release "themed" networks within our platform. Groups tackling similar types of projects – from education to energy; from permaculture to parks – should be enabled to follow what each other is up to, and to learn from one another, no matter where they are based.

Lastly, we want to enable more resources to flow to the community sector – and to match these with where the need is greatest. With cuts in public sector funding and austerity, there is ever-increasing demand from the community sector for resources to support the important work they do. At the same time there is growing focus from companies on supporting local initiatives, be it with funding, resources or allowing employees time off to volunteer locally. There is currently no simple mechanism connecting the two. Our nascent "Community Resourcing Tool" automates the brokerage role and provides a "marketplace" to bring together supply and demand, making it simpler and more efficient to get resources to cater for real project needs.

Authors

Nick Gardner is co-founder of Project Dirt. Nick's background is in social and environmental research, primarily for large government bodies and corporate clients. His work has ranged from evaluating major national lottery-funded programmes such as "Transforming Your Space", to auditing the Carbon Trust's Future Impact estimation tool for KPMG.

nick@projectdirt.com

Friederike Hanisch is Project Manager at Project Dirt. She works with Project Dirt's clients from the private, public and third sector, ensuring that their campaigns achieve maximum results. Previously she has worked in environmental research and other sustainability projects. Outside work, Friederike co-established a local community repairing initiative for electronic items.

friederike@projectdirt.com

THE ON SITE TRANSFORMER ENGINEERS

Rosh Engineering
http://rosh.co.uk

Award: Entrepreneurship (commercial)

The Mission

Rosh Engineering has been operating since 1981 and is a small family-run business with 30 staff. Rosh survives by being lean, flexible and innovative in its services to the large energy companies. Building upon the founder's experience in the transformer industry since the 1950s, Rosh Engineering has been involved in the extension of life and efficiency improvement of high-voltage equipment developing and promoting techniques for more than 30 years. Always keen to extol the benefits of retaining and improving equipment, Rosh Engineering now has a reputation for quality engineering with an emphasis on repair and re-use rather than retire and replace (see Appendix 1: Recycling Report).

Few changes have come to the principles of power transformers in the last 100 years. It is a metal box that does nothing but hum to most people and may appear boring to some. Paint it grey and run some electricity through it and the picture is complete. But without these grey boxes on every street corner and with bigger ones in substations around the world, the lights would go out and our 21st-century lifestyle would collapse. But Rosh Engineering can do exciting things with these grey boxes that hum.

The Challenge

A power transformer changes the voltage in the power network – high volts means low amps – and this means electricity can be transported around the country from power stations to homes efficiently, meaning very little of the generated energy is lost. But 400,000 volts are rather unpleasant if connected to little Johnny's train set, so transformers are used to bring the voltage down again over a number of stages on the way.

The size of the transformer is given a rating as to how much energy can pass through it in the network – such as 15 MVA – which stands for 15 Mega Volt Amps. As towns and cities grow and people plug in more gadgets many of these transformers are not big enough for the job. Often the transformers were installed in the 1950s, '60s and '70s when Apple and Blackberry were still fruit.

This rising demand would traditionally mean that the old transformer was scrapped and a new one installed. Transformers are made up of steel and copper and are filled with thousands of litres of oil, which can be recycled, but the whole process is very consumptive of energy in the process of scrapping the old and making and installing the new. And this old equipment invariably still has plenty of life in it.

Developing Sustainable Solutions

Rosh Engineering's technical expertise in transformers first proposed the potential to the energy companies that they could increase the rating of their transformers rather than scrapping them. Rosh Engineering can make a 15 MVA transformer into a 21 MVA transformer. It is a bit like making your 1600 cc car into a 2 litre car but without taking the engine out. This can be achieved at less than 5% of the cost of replacing the transformer, with less disruption to the power grid in terms of time unavailable for use, and the cherry on the top is it also helps saves some of the planet's finite resources.

Rosh Engineering's desire to avoid waste and make efficient use of natural resources in the whole process has driven us to promote this as the way forward for the energy industry and our planet. Working in a fiercely competitive industry we also appreciated that our customers needed to see not just environmental advantages but clear economic reasons to change the way they approached their asset management.

By fitting additional fans and pumps, and lots of technical expertise from the Rosh Engineering technical department, the opportunity to keep the lights on without making any bigger impact on the planet is booming. Big and small, from 1 MVA up to 300 MVA these boring grey boxes are being uprated. Their useful lives are being extended way beyond that which the designer originally conceived and being given another lease of life that could be another 20, 30 or even 40 years. That economic advantage makes a large impact.

Furthermore, the impact to our customers in replacing transformers has been significant in both management time and physical disruption. The modifications made by Rosh Engineering to achieve the end goal ensured most projects could be completed in one tenth of the time or less giving them a rapid and effective solution.

The process started because Rosh Engineering went back to the basics of how a transformer works, which has not changed in the last 100 years, and used fresh thinking to improve what already existed. It was not a matter of a new technological development, new software or new materials, but appreciating how transformers worked and applying knowledge to use finite resources more efficiently.

Experiences

One of the biggest challenges is overcoming the conservative nature of the industry, and convincing them that no adverse effects will be experienced in operation. Our industry is a notoriously cautious one, where innovation takes time to be adopted. Research, data from earlier projects, and professionalism in presenting the facts is overcoming the sceptics.

A railway company discovered that its transformers were not big enough due to the increasing frequency of trains, combined with the higher power demands of heavier trains – which were heavier to make them stronger in case of an accident. Combined with the installation of air conditioning, the railway company thought they would have to replace many transformers. While all transformers have a finite limit to the amount they can have their rating increased, Rosh Engineering was also able to analyse when the peaks occurred. Peak loads occurred during morning and evening rush hours. Monitoring these loads and temperatures with Rosh's knowledge of thermal load cycles meant a solution could be developed.

Spreading this knowledge is now paramount, while at the same time working with the owners and operators of transformers to maximize the benefit. Clients are won over by the benefits of not only short-term gains through the lower immediate financial costs and short turnaround times which lessen the vulnerability of the distribution system, but also by the forecasted benefits of longer equipment life and lower running costs.

As well as having a far smaller environmental footprint, we are now seeing more and more clients taking up the practices we preach.

The Future

Additional advances can now be worked on by the use of low noise fans to reduce noise pollution during this process, as well as deeper understanding of local climatic conditions. Typically, if a transformer is "working" hardest at night when temperatures in the atmosphere are lower, an even greater rating improvement can be achieved. This increases the opportunities and reduces the number of transformers that need to be scrapped.

On top of giving our customers a "bigger" transformer there is also a direct correlation between the heat at which a transformer operates, and its life expectancy. If you constantly drive a little Fiat 500 car at 100 mph it will not be long before it is worn out or will break down. A Ferrari on the other hand will manage to maintain this speed a lot longer and with fewer issues. Rosh Engineering turns Fiats into Ferraris. Albeit still painted grey, with the same gentle hum, they are making a significant impact in everyone's homes, and to the planet.

Appendix 1

Using historical data since 2011 to the present we can establish the following recycling, re-use and reduction of waste in the area of Transformer Life Extension and Enhancement.

The two most significant areas of waste in our operations are oil and metals.

Electrical Insulating Oil is mineral-based and obtained from non-renewable, carbon-based sources just like any other oil. Through proactive education and demonstration of the financial and environmental benefits to customers of re-using and regenerating oil, we have been able to greatly reduce our consumption of newly refined oil. Re-use and recycling has increased from 73% in 2010/2011 to 99.5% in 2013.

Oil

	Totals removed from customer equipment.	Oil sent specifically for recycling or reuse elsewhere	Oil regenerated and reused on site without removal (zero carbon impact)	Total sent for waste	Percentage recycled or reused (expressed against total)
2010 + 2011	82,495	27,080	33,400	22,015	73%
2012	91,577	8,177	80,000	3,400	96.2%
2013	126,355	33,755	92,000	600	99.5%
Notes		This oil is recycled for use in plastics, release agents, lubrication.	Oil that remains on customer sites and is reprocessed in specialized equipment and returned to service.	Oil which was sent for destruction for reasons such as contamination or hazardous elements within the oil.	
All amounts are litres. Totals for 2013 are not yet finalized. Figures quoted are correct as at 31st September 2013.						

Metals (steel, copper, aluminium, brass)

Also through our ability to enhance and extend the life of existing equipment through unique techniques and innovative thinking, we have been able to negate the need for scrapping equipment that is capable of providing many more years of service. Much of the equipment we are able to life extend contains copper which is highly consumptive of carbon resources in the production process.

If this equipment were to be scrapped it would of course be subject to recycling; however, this also consumes large amounts of energy in the process.

By eliminating the removal process entirely we can avoid the consumption of this energy.

This proactive approach has seen a percentage increase in material saved from 90% to 97.9%

Metals

	Potential amount of waste materials	New material used in projects	Material saved from waste stream	Figures quoted are based upon:
2011	1,000	100	900	Weight of equipment uprated or refurbished.
2012	1,200	110	1,090	
2013	7,300	150	7,150	
Notes	Estimated total amount of material which could have entered waste stream	Estimated amount of new materials used		Weight of new metals (steel, aluminium, copper) used in the work
All amounts are metric tonnes. Figure for 2013 is correct as at 31st September.				

Author

Ian Dormer has been Managing Director of Birtley, County Durham based specialist high-voltage engineering contractor Rosh Engineering Ltd since 1989. The company has grown from the front bedroom to operating out of a 1 acre site. Contracts are undertaken from Shetland in the North to the Channel Islands in the South, with many projects in the Netherlands, Ireland and occasionally further afield. The business focuses on a high-quality, safety-focused approach that adds value to its customer's business. Ian's personal commitment to health & safety led him to Chair a joint IoD/HSE oversight group on promoting positive leadership in the field. Ian is passionate about promoting the development of a positive business climate. This has resulted in past appointments to the

Board of Regional Development Agency, ONE North East, through to becoming National Chairman of The Institute of Directors.

info@rosh.co.uk   0191 410 6300

PleaseCycle (now Yomp)
http://yomp.co

Award: Entrepreneurship (social)

The Mission

At Yomp we provide gamification software designed to create healthier, happier and more sustainable organizations.

We help corporates and local authorities engage with their audiences by using a number of behavioural change methodologies, which is key in encouraging more people to make the switch to more sustainable travel methods.

Yomp provides client-branded online and mobile portals allowing users to track their journeys, see what CO_2 their sustainable journeys have saved compared to driving and how much money sustainable travel can save them. Yomp aims to help people understand the impact their travel choices have on the wider environment. In turn this allows organizations and local authorities to specifically report on the reduced impact their employees or residents have on the wider area, providing key corporate and social responsibility statistics.

Large cities around the world are the centres of innovation, growth and development. They have to become the catalyst in making the world economy more sustainable. Their use of technology is instrumental in reaching people on an individual level and encouraging behavioural change.

The impending obesity epidemic, increase in sedentary lifestyles and dietary issues justifies our call to shift transport policy from sedentary to active travel. The benefits of physical activity, however, go much further than weight loss and have the potential to save billions of pounds per year in healthcare costs (Department of Health, 2013). Equally, the Clean Air for Europe initiative and other EU legislation seek to improve air quality, largely by reducing the emissions caused by vehicle use.

The Challenge

Transport for London reported an 8% growth in cycling during 2010 which is the equivalent of an additional 45,000 journeys on top of the half million, plus journeys being done by bike each day. With the percentage of people in the UK also reporting to walk for at least 10 minutes continuously once a week being around 90% of the population, why is it proving so hard to get people out of their cars? With 24 million journeys being done in London – not to mention similar cities around the world each day – how can we get more people to think more about their travel methods?

In 2014 we partnered with Dentsu Aegis Network (DAN), one of the largest media umbrellas in the world to look at this question. DAN wanted to reduce their indirect emissions, including the carbon footprint related to their employees' commute. To achieve this goal they decided to engage people around sustainable behaviour beyond the office walls. DAN's aim was to raise the number of people walking, running or cycling to work with at least 10% engagement in selected offices.

That's where Yomp stepped in – our digital platform and smartphone app engages corporate staff through rewarding and incentivizing sustainable travel.

Developing Sustainable Solutions

We launched Yomp in May 2014 in 45 DAN offices in 9 countries, inviting just over 5,000 employees to take part. The target agreed with DAN was to sign up at least 10 per cent of them. The countries and offices represented a mix of cycling, running and walking cultures – from the Netherlands to Canada and Italy to Australia.

Dentsu Aegis Network planned to achieve behaviour shift through utilizing a branded Yomp portal (and app) to encourage employees to cycle, run and walk to work in return for small rewards and recognition. Whether people are seasoned cyclists, runners, and walkers or just wanted to give it a go, Yomp's online platform inspires users to join colleagues and rewards them for every mile they record. Users were able to access top tips, plan safe routes to the office, log mileage, see carbon savings and compete against colleagues from other offices on the leaderboard.

Figure 1: Dentsu Aegis Network's Yomp portal

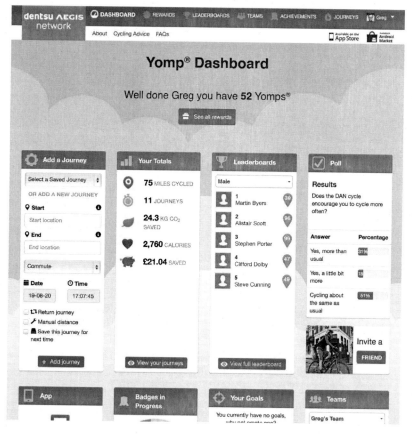

During the months of May and June, 602 employees (more than our 10 per cent of the targeted audience) across the network logged just over 7,000 green commutes to and from work, covering more than 30,000 miles.

As part of the Yomp system users were offered a mixture of intrinsic rewards (improved fitness, healthy competition with colleagues, team formation and interaction) and extrinsic rewards (virtual trophies and badges as well as physical rewards such as a coffee). We saw a total of 436 individuals redeem rewards distributed across 9 countries: these ranged from free ice creams in Germany to free tea/coffee in London. 134 people opted to donate their miles to charity resulting in a donation to SOS Save the Children by Dentsu Aegis Network.

The environmental benefit has materialized in an estimated 10 metric tonnes CO_2 emissions avoided compared to DAN employees' normal commute. Equally important, the people who engaged with the programme got healthier: the 7,000 green journeys equal approximately one million calories burnt. Yomp also helped raise the awareness of the longer-term environmental impacts of an individual's commute, with 30% of users reporting that they cycled more now than before the initiative.

Of the total registrants there was a complete spectrum of users from those that rarely actively commute to those that often actively travel; 40% mentioned they cycle "often", 30% "sometimes" and, interestingly, 30% "rarely cycled" before the launch. The last two segments were of particular interest to DAN, since these were the people being asked to make the largest change in their behaviour.

The quality of audience engagement is also evident in the open rates of newsletters sent weekly. Throughout the scheme emails received over a 40% open rate, showing a high engagement with both Yomp and the DAN wellness scheme.

Additionally, by commuting in a healthier way, DAN employees had a higher potential for being more productive at work with fewer sick days, as documented in various research studies about the positive connection between health and employee efficiency.

Figure 2: Bespoke Facebook infographic presenting the impact of the campaign

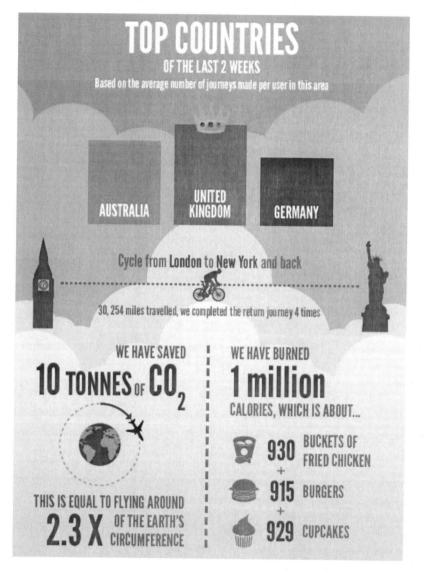

Yomp was an innovative project in the way it used digital technology to affect 602 people's behaviour. First of all, the use of a bespoke online portal and accompanying app ensured that each registrant was reached on their most personal device, which travelled from home to the office and back every day. On top of that, leaderboards allowed offices to engage and compete with one-another to see which county was recording the most journeys, all for a good cause. The dynamic Facebook app (Figure 2) created specifically for DAN kept everyone in the loop as to the total collective achievement, broken down into more visceral statistic, i.e. number of times travelled around the world.

Experiences

How people behave is often hard to understand and can be affected by a vast number of different factors therefore behavioural change can be difficult to achieve. Successful implementation of gamification (the use of game elements and mechanics in a typically non-gaming environment) requires a number of key objectives to be outlined in order to target the desired behavioural change.

Step 1: Define main objectives
Yomp's main objective is to get more people to travel in a sustainable manner more often.

Step 2: Delineate target behaviours

It is important to focus on the desired behavioural change in order to put the correct means of measurement in place. Since behaviours and metrics are best considered together, Yomps's target behaviours are concrete and specific. Some of the examples include:

- Sign up for an account on the website,
- Log cycling, running or walking trips at least once a week,
- Create a goal,
- Take part in an active commute competition,
- Form or join a team,
- Share your experiences on Facebook or Twitter.

Step 3: Describe the users

It is important to remember that real people use these systems. It sounds obvious, but it is easily overlooked and something that it is very hard to rectify. It is important to know who the users are and anticipate and understand what their needs are and will be moving forward. It is important that the information captured is carefully analysed to provide the most relevant experience to users throughout the lifecycle of the product and future iterations.

Step 4: Devise activity/engagement cycles

There are two kinds of "activity cycle" used on the Yomp platform: engagement loops and progression stairs. Engagement loops describe, at micro level, what users do, why they do it, and what the system does in response.

Progression stairs give a macro perspective on the "player's" journey. It is crucial to get these cycles right as getting them wrong means you risk undoing any behavioural change already achieved and potentially losing the interest of the user full-time.

Step 5: Don't forget the fun

Before a gamification solution is implemented it is important to take a step back and as a simple question: is it fun? Fun is not easy to predict, but the best way to tell if the system is fun is to build it, test it and refine it though a rigorous design system. Yomp have gone through a number of phases in order to produce products that work for the specific audiences they are asked to cater for.

Step 6: Deploy the appropriate tools

The last stage is to pick the appropriate game mechanics, components and elements and deliver them through an effective mechanism. Yomp are very careful about which elements are selected, constantly bearing in mind that the user experience should be fun and motivating to encourage increased usage and ultimately behaviour change. It is a refined balance of various elements that helps create a successful system.

The Future

Gamification could be hugely influential when it comes to affecting people's habits. The volume of investment going into the sector is a clear indication that the appetite both in terms of consumers and suppliers/employers/authorities is growing. With people's travel habits beginning to positively shift, gamification shows signs of being an important method of assisting the change and that it is not simply a phase.

For future initiatives, it is evident that Yomp cannot be run in all countries due to cultural differences and idiosyncrasies in city infrastructures. It is important to carefully understand the specific country before launching a Yomp platform. An example of this is the intended launch in a DAN Brazilian organization: cycling was not deemed safe enough within the proximity of the offices so encouraging this would be potentially dangerous and very counterproductive. Additionally, in hotter climates like Asia, it is impossible to cycle or run to work because of the heat and humidity. For these countries Yomp could expand beyond cycling, running and walking to include other modes of transport such as public transport and carpooling or even other health-related activities to improve staff wellbeing.

The images featured in the article belong to Yomp®. All rights reserved.

In this article we also used the following resources:
- Video lectures from Coursera's MOOC "Gamification"
- "For the Win" by Kevin Werbach

Authors

Prior to joining Yomp, **Greg Drach** founded Inscribe Media, an advertising media company targeting students at the UK's top-tier universities. Greg's skills and expertise range from product development, to projects and processes management. Having completed with distinction a Penn University course in gamification and behavioural change, Greg is Yomp's expert on improving engagement and effectiveness of the software.

greg@yomp.co

Crispin Moller has 6 years of client and account management experience from B2B gaming and IT sectors. He's worked with a wide variety of companies, from large multinational corporates through to national and international media organizations. Crispin brings to Yomp a wealth of B2B SaaS experience – especially in areas of client-liaison and "playbooks" for user engagement / retention.

crispin@yomp.co

Core Arts

http://corearts.co.uk

Award: Greening the Third Sector

The Mission

Core Landscapes is one of a number of entrepreneurial ventures set up by Core Arts, an award-winning charity committed to promoting positive mental health.

Core Arts' base in Hackney, East London, is a user-led Creative Training Centre with a yearly referred membership of over 360 adults with severe and enduring mental health issues. Core Arts members are supported through creative programmes (art, music, multimedia, creative writing, drama and horticulture) to develop their confidence, self-esteem and skills. The associated social enterprises offer members training and work experience providing a bridge into social and economic independence.

Core Landscapes focuses on bringing about social change locally through inclusive and participatory environmental projects. It provides high-quality horticultural services engaging a disenfranchised group of mental health service users who are at the heart of the enterprise's planning, development and delivery.

The Challenge

Core Arts Horticultural Projects are transforming temporary sites for local growing and greening use through the use of recycled and upcycled land, building and plant waste for community benefit. We empower communities to develop these temporary vacant sites and facilitate partnerships to improve public space. The project focuses on encouraging wellbeing and promoting social change locally through participatory environmental projects. Core Arts has facilitated three projects using vacant meanwhile land, unused land and roofs for community benefits whilst awaiting regeneration.

- The Growing PlacE16
- Silver Town Way E16
- Core Arts Gardens E9

The benefits include reducing ecological footprints:

1. Reducing waste generation by re-using and upcycling end of commercial jobs' waste such as sand, gravel, paving stones, wood, plants and trees and using it to transform derelict land.
2. Regenerating plants obtained from the end of gardening contracts and reusing them for community benefit.
3. Local growing of plants and vegetables in unused brownfill and toxic land.

Canning Town images: Core Arts Landscape Project (1)

Summary of the "Greening the Grey" aims

- Engaging hard-to-reach communities especially those suffering mental health issues in greening and growing and thereby improving health and wellbeing.
- Improving localities by using meanwhile temporary spaces to provide growing spaces that enhance the

disused sites into productive community growing spaces.
- Help reduce social isolation through working with others
- Engage people of all ages in the management of their community green space and improving their local environment
- Engaging hard-to-reach communities in all aspects of beekeeping and the provision of equipment and hives.

Developing Sustainable Solutions

Core Landscapes was initially set up in 2003 and its achievements to date include:

Developing Core Arts training in horticulture

Core Arts set up an initiative to manage a number of gardening contracts near its base in the London Borough of Hackney in 2003. Core Arts members work within the Core Landscape team gaining confidence, practical training and experience in basic gardening skills, green space management and garden design.

The redesign, re-landscaping and long-term maintenance of Homerton Hospital's gardens

Since 2004 Core Landscapes has been contracted to maintain and develop the hospital's courtyard gardens. Using innovative design and interesting planting Core has redesigned and improved two of the courtyards. The gardens

provide a healing natural environment for hospital users and provide ongoing training and work experience for mental health
service users.

Winning a contract with Ground Work East (2006)

Funding from USB Bank enabled Core Landscapes to involve local children in planting 400 trees and growing a vegetable garden in Homerton Grove Adventure Playground. The project increased the children's awareness of environmental issues and land management and encouraged local biodiversity.

Commissioning the Boulder in Mabley Green

Core Arts invited the artist John Franklin to place this ambitious public realm sculpture as a local landmark in one of Hackney's parks. Climbing on the rock is actively encouraged and, in partnership with the Castle Climbing Centre (see page 72), Core ran a number of "bouldering" workshops and events in the park. The project was funded by REAP and is part of the regeneration plans within Hackney which aim to benefit neighbourhoods which hosted the Olympic Games.

Winning the Green Pennant Award for Core Arts Garden in 2008/2009

Core Arts Garden has turned a derelict site adjacent to Core Arts Centre into a permanent resource. The project provides a base for extending Core Arts creative training programme through horticultural classes, garden design and volunteering. The project was listed as one of the best community managed green spaces in 2008 and the

Core Arts & Landscapes' inclusive approach to green space design, recycling and reclaiming materials from waste to positive use, programming and management means its projects are sustainable and contribute to the wider community and neighbourhood development goals for local places.

The Core Arts Horticulture project's awards include:

- "London in Bloom" certificate of excellence
- "Hackney in Bloom" certificate of excellence
- A Green Pennant Award for best community garden
- The Growing localities award for reclaiming and developing wasteland

Experiences

Outcomes so far include:

- 26 disadvantaged community groups participated, 27 professional partners, 150 volunteers, community audiences of 1,500 at events.
- Landscape Social Enterprise established and commercial contracts won.
- One website set up www.core-landscapes.com,.
- Two publications written:
  - A 35-page colour book was produced that evaluated and will now be used to advertise the idea and service. "Core Landscapes @ Growing PlacE16: How to use temporary sites for

local growing, social enterprise and community benefit".
- A second 4-page pamphlet was created to act as a fundraising information tool for potential partners: "The Growing PlacE16: How to utilize temporary sites for community benefit and social enterprise".

These are available to download on our website: www.core-landscapes.co.uk.

Our key challenge was that the move from one site to another took more time, and was more expensive, than predicted. When moving to the next space we have reached agreements with developers that will be moving to our current site, that they would move the large items on site free-of-charge as part of their match-funding of the project.

The Future

The project's temporary nature has encouraged exciting levels of experiment and growing spaces have been set up with a view to "moving on". The approach shows the immediate and positive impact of occupying problem sites, and the possibility of relocation. Positive outcomes for individuals, local groups and partnerships also indicate a longer-term potential that could be harnessed to support community development.

Our role provides practical ways for small local community groups to access partners to engage in the project and gives the wider community a point of contact allowing unplanned and exciting partnerships to form. The operational success of the social enterprise underpins all our activity in Canning Town and elsewhere, allowing us to re-invest in our members and partner communities in the role of mentors and facilitators. The project is led by Nursery Manager for two days a week to manage the project, and relies on volunteers and community involvement so it is low cost and replicable across the UK.

The recent downturn in the economy means that a number of planned schemes have stalled and sites cleared for development may remain dormant for some time. This presents a real opportunity for community groups to access these temporary sites so they can be used for community benefit whist developers wait for an upturn.

Canning Town images: Core Arts Landscape Project (2)

Contact Details

mail@corearts.co.uk   020 8533 3500

Abundance
www.abundancegeneration.com
Award: Sustainable Finance

The Mission

Abundance is a FCA-regulated online investment platform that enables anybody in the local community, UK or European Economic Area (EEA) to invest in renewable energy projects with just £5.

The Abundance mission is twofold and gives people what we call a truly "win win" investment opportunity.

Firstly, we want to give people control of their money. With regular updates on projects and the energy generated, it is easy and clear for investors to see for themselves exactly how their money is earning them an income.

Secondly, we want to democratize the financing of renewable energy while simultaneously increasing engagement with and support for renewables in order to accelerate the transition to a low carbon economy. Not only does this put power – both literally and figuratively – into the hands of the people, it also helps to create a greener, cleaner place to live for everyone.

As with any investment product there are risks, and it is important to remember that any return on investments depends on the success of the individual project. They are long-term investments that may not be readily realizable throughout their term and returns can be variable.

The Challenge

The challenge involved initially was obtaining authorization from the FSA (now the FCA) in 2011. Abundance was the first UK crowdfunding site to achieve this, which is testament to our commitment to making renewable energy investment open to all as it was first deemed too complex to offer to "retail investors". Over 16 months, Abundance educated the FSA on the relatively low-risk nature of renewable energy and proved that, if done correctly, it provided an attractive investment opportunity to mainstream investors.

A further challenge has been to demonstrate to people that renewable energy investment doesn't need to be complicated or daunting and conveying this message to the wider public, who may never have considered investing directly into renewable energy before, or indeed ever made an investment at all.

Developing Sustainable Solutions

We have addressed various challenges in a number of ways.

Setting up a crowdfunding platform was the first challenge. It was vital to create a website where the idea of

Abundance and what it could offer were clearly articulated, while keeping costs to a minimum so that we could offer the low £5 minimum investment and offer competitive fees to developers.

With the platform set up, it was necessary to find projects to offer for investment. Thankfully this has not been one of the more difficult challenges. Since launching our first project in July 2012, we have raised finance for nine projects, with a number due to come online over the next few months. There is a strong appetite among developers for using the Abundance model to raise finance, as we enable them to engage the local community by offering them a stake in the financial return of the project. Furthermore, with the impact of the recession seeing banks restrict lending, it has not been easy for smaller developers to obtain bank funding. Thus we are solving a set of problems – financial and community support/participation – within the renewables industry, in turn enabling more projects to come to fruition and accelerate the transition to a more sustainable UK.

However, finding projects is not the end of the challenge. In order to ensure the full amount required is raised, we have needed to continually build brand awareness. This has been achieved in a number of ways, primarily through PR around alternative finance. Doing something totally unique and new to the alternative finance sector, let alone the broader traditional finance sector, has given us a good angle from which to pitch to journalists in both mainstream and niche publications. The result has been extensive coverage across a broad range of publications, including *The Sunday Times*, BBC and *The Guardian*. This has the combined effect of alerting people to our business while also bringing alternative finance into the mainstream consciousness.

Our strong management team, whose previous experience includes both traditional and alternative finance, helped to ensure that we had the knowledge necessary to be pioneers in the alternative finance sector.

With the financial industry in the UK heavily regulated (and rightly so) for the protection of investors, it was an uphill struggle to gain authorization from the FSA. Over a period of 16 months we worked with them and educated them on the risks and rewards of crowdfunding and direct renewable energy investment. When we gained approval, we became the first crowdfunding platform to be regulated by the FSA, setting a precedent for all those that came after us. What was most significant though, was that with approval we were able to open renewable energy investment to all and thereby create what we call democratic finance, which makes it possible for anybody to make an investment and earn an income no matter how much or how little they have.

Experiences

There have been numerous valuable lessons learned along the way so far, and we expect to learn many more as time goes on.

Arguably the most important lesson learned on the Abundance journey has been of the need to educate people about renewable energy investment and how renewable energy in their local area can benefit them.

Most people have almost no experience of making direct investments into renewables and, as such, do not think they have the necessary skill to choose low-risk, "good" options. This leaves banks, pension providers and the like in control of a lot of money and investment decisions. What we have achieved is a way of communicating potential risks and reward in a clear, simple manner that helps to give people the confidence to invest.

As well as this, many people have a fear of having renewable energy "thrust" upon them or their local landscape. In partnership with the developers we work with, we have been proactive in attending planning consultations and notifying local residents of projects in their local area that are open for investment through Abundance. This has led to a number of local people investing, giving them a vested interest in the performance of the technology as well as keeping some of the profits from the energy generated in the local community. Many of our projects also have the added benefit of a community fund, or lowering electricity bills for schools and other public service buildings, which again enhances local support for and engagement with projects as there is a clear benefit to having renewable energy.

The low minimum investment of just £5 has also been a success, as people who are new to investing in renewables are often happy to invest a small sum to experience for themselves how Abundance works. Once they have held the investment for a little time and experienced receiving cash returns or interest payments, confidence increases and a number become repeat customers who go on to invest in other projects.

The biggest roadblock was obtaining FSA authorization. Happily, this happened in 2011. Since then there have not so much been roadblocks as a series of hurdles, which is common in any business. In the renewable energy and financial services industries this has meant, for example, occasional project delays or technical issues.

We feel that the most important lesson we could impart to others is to support others in your industry and forge lasting relationships with them, as each company will have a different experience and be able to offer advice or a new way of looking at something that you may have missed. Being able to draw on the experience of others and turn to them when something doesn't go as planned, as well as having others with whom to share your successes, really is invaluable.

The Future

Abundance has lots of exciting projects in the pipeline, including forays into technologies such as hydro and biomass. Our projects are also rather larger than when we first started out, not least because we have more new visitors and members coming to the site and signing up who are keen to invest.

Looking further ahead, our plan is to eventually offer socially responsible investment into not only renewable energy but also other local infrastructure projects, such as social housing, leisure centres or even schools. Opening up these sectors to retail investors rather than private institutions will do much the same for other local infrastructure as it has for renewables, making development more inclusive and democratic by sharing the financial and social benefits amongst a large number of people rather than a few private backers or banks.

We are also very excited by the prospect of peer-to-peer ISAs, which would benefit savers, communities and the environment by encouraging more people to put at least some of their money into an investment that offers much more than just a financial return.

Author

Karina Sidenius is Marketing Executive at Abundance

www.abundanceinvestment.com   020 3475 8666   @AbundanceGen

Co-oproduct.org
...a revolution in the making

Co-oproduct CIC
www.co-oproduct.org

Award: Responsible Waste Management & Social Entrepreneurship

The Mission

Co-oproduct CIC is a community-driven educational "hub" for sustainable and ethical practice. We encourage responsible behaviour in a number of ways, but we are guided by our two main aims. All of our activities and efforts are directed towards this positive end:

1. To use a design-led approach to champion new ways of improving the afterlife of products through the reuse and repair of household packaging and everyday waste materials.
2. To pilot a new, community-based model of product design, which supports everyday people to openly share their reuse and repair ideas, maximizing knowledge for all.

We work with schools, colleges and universities in the UK and abroad. By running workshops, competitions, writing projects and learning materials, we are helping to deliver completely new education in ethical and sustainable design practice.

The Challenge

Co-oproduct.org is an online portal for the free sharing of product design ideas focusing on design for reuse, repair and longer-life products and packaging. The organization was incorporated in October 2008 and the web portal was launched on March 19, 2012. The main focus of our work to date has been to develop and maintain an online portal, which supports the open and free sharing of desirable MIY (Make-It-Yourself) products. At the very heart of this work, is the drive to find innovative methods of re-using existing packaging and household waste materials, eliminating (as far as possible) the need for further processing and manufacture.

We see current production models as outdated and a major, unnecessary contributor to environmental damage. Though our work, we aim to provide crowd-sourced/people-driven, real-world examples of alternatives. With our focus on home manufacturing, education and knowledge acquisition, through openness and sharing culture, we seek to empower people all over the world to take action and make positive changes to their own consumption habits.

Developing Sustainable Solutions

The Co-oproduct web portal is a free resource where users can publish and obtain instructions on how to repair, make and create products from waste materials. Co-oproduct promotes and supports community collaboration and the free, public sharing of knowledge. All Co-oproduct Make-It-Yourself instructions listed on the web portal are made available to the public for free non-commercial use under a Creative Commons Licence.

We choose to operate our efforts digitally, through our website and social media channels, since this eradicates the need for many existing and outdated models of production (such as transportation of goods, for example). Additionally, our online presence means that we have a much greater reach to people all over the world, which is key to successful innovation models. In this way, our project does not need to produce goods because we are facilitating the production of "transformed attitudes" and new ideas for sustainable consumption, through democratic engagement and positive real-world examples.

Our current database consists of over 700 products that can be made with post-consumer packaging/household waste (many of which can be easily made in the home), eradicating the need for raw materials and high-energy production methods. Furthermore, we are also working on more advanced home manufacturing solutions for high-end technical/electronic consumer products. These solutions will be developed and delivered in the same way.

At the time of writing, we engage 1,087 registered members on our website, 1.9k Facebook, 548 Twitter and 271

Pinterest followers. Approximately 50% of our audience are design students, 25% designer-makers/hobbyists and the remaining 25% are professional designers and academics/educators.

Our website receives regular traffic from 139 different countries of the world. Of the 139 different countries who regularly visit us, the top 10 of our last quarter were: UK, US, Canada, Nicaragua, Germany, Australia, Poland, Argentina, Spain and India. Nottingham and London are our most popular cities totaling 20% of all visits during this period.

Through these channels, our visitors and members collectively engage with over 700 projects and 1,000s of tutorials showcasing and promoting examples of re-use, repair and longer-life products and packaging use and solutions. All projects and tutorials are user-submitted and access to these projects and tutorials is always open, transparent and free.

Given the demographic diversity, the global scale of our user-engagement and our resource database/s, our efforts make a healthy and positive sustainable contribution to the wellbeing of the UK and the other 139 countries that we regularly impact.

This is part of our ongoing project, using a design-led approach to take action against the problem with waste in the UK and abroad.

"Plastic Bag Mesh Dress" by Naomi Andrews, Chloe Bampton, Annie Edgerton.

Image © Life Photographic (www.lifephotographic.co.uk)

Makeup: Clare Newman; Hair: Anthony Holland; Model: Marta Rembielinska

Willow Farm Primary School: workshop

"Cyclehangers" by Oliver Staiano

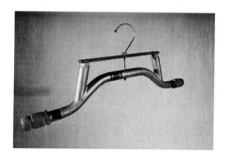

Experiences

Our organization is unconventional and, for this reason, our approach is difficult for many to fully grasp. We do not promote consumption models through the buying and selling of goods; rather we encourage home manufacturing techniques and resourcefulness through education and knowledge attainment, often resulting in the repair and re-use of existing goods with minimal negative impact on the environment. To our knowledge, we are the only UK Community Interest Company that adopts this innovate model of operation which is perhaps, in direct contrast to more popular and well documented strategies of "designed obsolescence".

For this reason, we face many difficult challenges when trying to integrate our business model into current economic and consumer structures. Understandably, our approach doesn't always appeal to existing businesses, who operative mainly through the creation and targeting of markets, in order to sell more products.

This is why we are working hard in the education sector, the local community and by building relationships with brands and manufacturers in order to contextualize what we do, so that these cultures can begin to understand, then embrace the need to engage with our strategy for a much more sustainable and ethical future.

Between July 2013 and March 2014, we received four awards for our work.

The Future

We openly and freely publish detailed instructions on our website and through our social media channels showing anyone, anywhere, how to replicate the work that we do.

In addition, we also provide consultancy and software tools to encourage and enable community engagement, sharing and interaction. This can be seen throughout our web portal, but particularly in our community area.

Co-oproduct exists for the sole purpose of sharing and replicating the sustainable and ethical work that we do. We do this in an effort to minimize the negative impact on the environment caused by current models of consumption and production. We are a sensitive and proactive organization and pride ourselves on our mature approach to developing and promoting alternative models of sustainable, ethical and economical practice.

In January 2015, we will launch our new website, which will expand our current work to include "design for longer life", "design for repair" and "design for recycling". As a result of this, we will be engaging our audience with our most recent ground-breaking work into "closed loop" home manufacturing/3D printing, as well as continuing to provide all of our existing free tools, services and information.

Authors

Tracy Cordingley is Creative Director & Co-Founder at Co-oproduct. Tracy has a first degree in Interior Architecture, and studied MA Industrial Design at Central Saint Martin's College of Art & Design, London. Since graduating in 2001 she has worked across a wealth of different design practices, from Furniture and Product Design to Graphics and New Media. Her main interests lie in new technological developments and the changing interdisciplinary boundaries of the product design profession. In recent years Tracy has become particularly interested in Open Design and the potential these new community-based models have to reshape traditional working methods and practices of design. Tracy is a part-time Senior Lecturer in Product Design at Nottingham Trent University.

tracy@co-oproduct.org

Jamie Billing is Technical Director & Co-Founder at Co-oproduct. Jamie spent three years studying Foundation at Falmouth Art College in Cornwall, he has a BA (Hons.) in Design Futures from Newport School of Art and Design and graduated from MA Industrial Design at Central St Martin's in 2001. Jamie has worked as a consultant in Product Design, Graphics, Branding and New Media and currently works part-time as a Senior Lecturer in Product Design at Nottingham Trent University. Jamie has a utopian vision for product design and he believes that products, ideas and the associated knowledge should be openly shared, benefiting everyone... not just a few individuals and shareholders.

jamie@co-oproduct.org

Nampak Plastics

www.nampak.com

Award: Responsible Waste Management

The Mission

Nampak Plastics is a subsidiary of Nampak, a large South African packaging organization specializing in a wide range of packaging solutions. Nampak Plastics is the UK's leading manufacturer of High Density Polyethylene (HDPE) bottles, with nine sites across the UK and Northern Ireland. It manufactures around two billion bottles per annum and currently employs around 600 employees.

However, what sets Nampak apart from other companies is the lengths that it goes to in order to ensure that its waste management procedures are the very best that they can be. Indeed, sustainability is at the heart of the Nampak business: from its commitment to creating innovative, lightweight packaging solutions to staff understanding of how its manufacturing processes impact on the environment.

Nampak has launched a product which helps to save 34,000 tonnes of carbon each year and reduced the overall amount of carbon it produces by 16% (equivalent to taking 12,000 cars off the road). These milestones – and many more – have been attained through a variety of different work streams, including product innovation and working processes.

The Challenge

With three billion plastic milk bottles purchased every year in the UK, it is the most widely used item of packaging in the country. Therefore, any breakthrough in the design of the milk bottle can have a huge impact.

An iconic piece of packaging, the plastic milk bottle had been the same shape for more than two decades. However, to achieve lower weight, less waste and fewer tonnes of material used, a new solution was needed. In the past, lightweighting of plastic bottles had been achieved by simply using less material, but there is a limit to how thin the bottle walls can be whilst being "fit for purpose". It was clear that a more radical change was required.

Added to this, a dramatic shift in industry standards meant that internal processes needed to be refined. New standards were set to ensure businesses would have to make significant savings on energy and material consumption, and also reduce waste, through revised existing frameworks.

Nampak's Infini bottle

Developing Sustainable Solutions

Product innovation

Because of the huge impact design can have, in 2012, after a four-year process, Nampak launched its multi-award-winning Infini bottle – one of the world's lightest and strongest plastic milk bottles. To improve on an already successful product was a tall order for Nampak but in 2013 the company did two things:

Firstly, Nampak created the world's lightest four-pint HDPE bottle. Weighing only 32 g, it is a 20% material saving on the standard version and if it was to become the bottle of choice, it would reduce the overall amount of resin used in UK milk packaging by 10,000 tonnes.

Secondly, Nampak created a version of the Infini bottle which includes up to 30% recycled HDPE, double that of any other milk bottle on the market. This achievement means that the target of reaching the 30% mark by 2015 – set by Dairy UK and Defra in the Dairy Road Map – was reached two years ahead of schedule, and it is estimated that this move will save the industry some 25,000 tonnes of material yearly.

These two moves combined could result in 35,000 tonnes of material saved every year and will also herald significant carbon savings across the industry.

Working processes

Nampak refined its internal working practices to conform to the internationally recognized environmental standard ISO 14001 which, since its implementation, has brought about benefits including savings on consumption of energy and materials, a reduced cost of waste management and a framework for continuous improvement.

Furthermore, Nampak's environmental policy is supported by an "Aspects and Impacts" register, which is used to trace and assess each area of improvement. This has been used successfully to achieve goals on areas such as the lightweighting of the Infini bottle, the amount of recycled material going into Nampak's bottles and energy reduction initiatives including automated machine shut-off.

Nampak had a company-wide drive to enhance sustainability through recycling and waste management. It appointed "Carbon Champions" at each of its nine sites who were responsible for ensuring waste recovery and recycling best practice on a day-to-day basis.

Nampak organizes regular training courses for its staff, to provide them with an all-encompassing understanding of the company's environmental concerns. A scheme is also in place to reward staff who suggest ideas to drive environmental improvement. Ideas are encouraged from across the business and new initiatives that have derived from this approach include scanning in the warehouse to improve accuracy and traceability, and improving air conditioning systems in order to create a better working environment for both shop floor workers and machinery.

Experiences

In producing Infini, Nampak has overcome some difficult roadblocks. As well as the design elements which Nampak spent four years developing with tests and trials, the team also faced challenges in securing enough recycled material.

Overcoming these, the company's approach has had a myriad benefits to the business and the industry as a whole.

Employee culture

Nampak adopts a flat, "matrix" staff structure which has meant that through encouraging staff to suggest ideas to drive environmental improvement, a range of new initiatives have been implemented. The company's commitments to encouraging its workforce to get involved in all aspects of the business was recognized when Nampak received the accolade of overall winner in the Chartered Institute of Personnel Development (CIPD) awards, as well as winning the Employment Engagement Category.

Some of the engagement initiatives launched to ensure employees are motivated and have a positive experience at work include an Employee of the Month award and suggestion scheme; a buddy system for new employees, and an annual staff Excellence Awards, where the winners are nominated by their colleagues in a number of categories. Nampak also offers Institute of Leadership and Management development programmes – resulting in all managers, at all levels, receiving support in delivering their roles.

Importantly, however, Nampak's commitment to people doesn't start and finish with those at the company. Employees are encouraged to work with local students to teach them about the environment and sustainability, and employees are encouraged to take part in many charitable events too.

In-plant arrangement

Nampak recommends that, like them, their customers adopt an "in-plant" arrangement, which means that blow moulding equipment (used to manufacture milk bottles) is in a facility adjacent to the bottle filler rather than at a separate site. Seven out of Nampak's nine sites are "in-plant" facilities and, at the largest of these, CO_2 emissions relative to resin usage have been reduced by 8.5% in the last three years.

This has two key benefits. Firstly, it helps to reduce the requirement for "bagging" the bottles to be sent to the dairy and then "debagging" at the dairy, reducing the quantities of LDPE film required for the process. Secondly, it eliminates road transportation of empty bottles, saving on average more than one million miles a year and related CO_2 emissions. For example, at Nampak's Foston "in-plant" facility, bottles now move between the two buildings on conveyor belts rather than wagons – meaning that forklift truck emissions and diesel consumption have been cut.

The Future

The achievements with Infini are only just the beginning, and Nampak has strong ambitions for the future.

Not only has the success of the Infini bottle propelled Nampak to the forefront of the UK's milk packaging market, this year it is anticipated that the Infini bottle will be responsible for significant international growth of the business. Nampak's Infini bottle is expanding into other sectors, such as the detergent sector, as well as moving abroad into Australian and New Zealand markets in 2014, with discussions in progress with licensing partners in the US, European, Asian and African markets.

Nampak is already looking to beat the Dairy Roadmap 2020 target of 50% rHDPE, with bottles already in trials. Added to this, the unique design of the Infini bottle means it can be lightweighted further in the future too. The annual carbon reduction that Infini achieves is equivalent to the same weight as 50,000 Mini Coopers, and now over 800,000,000 have now been sold. It is one of the world's most decorated pieces of packaging with six awards on a national and international scale and to find out more, visit www.infinibottle.com or follow @infinibottle on Twitter.

Author

Eric Collins, Managing Director of Nampak Plastics, has helped the company and its staff to champion and implement good environmental practice. It is with Eric's oversight that Nampak, with input from across the business, created the Infini bottle – the world's lightest 4 pint (2.27 litre) 32 g bottle, which contains up to 20% less material than a standard bottle, and up to 30% recycled material. This, in turn, saves 34,000 tonnes of carbon each year and reduced the overall amount of carbon it produces by 16% (equivalent to taking 12,000 cars off the road). These breakthroughs could have only been achieved through the company's commitment to technological advancements, and sustainable packaging.

Castle Climbing Centre
www.castle-climbing.co.uk

Award: Responsible Waste Management/Sustainable Food

The Mission

The Castle Climbing Centre is a dedicated climbing centre with over 2,500 m^2 of climbing walls spread over five floors and is one of the busiest climbing centres in Europe. The climbing is housed within a grade 2 listed, Victorian building which was formerly a water pumping station.

Back in 2008, with the business well established and his family growing up, Steve Taylor (the Castle's CEO) had more time to really look at what was happening in the world, he read up on climate change and the problems we're facing, and decided that now was the time to act.

Let's be honest with ourselves. All of us are guilty of talking about what needs to change, but not many of us actually stand up and take action and to such an extent that those actions cause a ripple effect, changing other people's perceptions. Steve is one such man and he set about creating a positive example. He approached the Castle's core managers and the board of directors with his thoughts about the state of the planet and his plans to make some changes to the business.

The Challenge

The hardest challenge in any business or community is to change the culture. But that is exactly what we needed to do to move to a more sustainable way of living. The Castle's key strategies for managing change have been to involve people and communicate everything we're trying to achieve effectively. Our staff are the main drivers for change because without their commitment we couldn't have achieved what we have and it is them that keep the whole project moving forwards.

We also have to remember that first and foremost we're a climbing centre and people come here to climb, not to be bombarded with "hippy ideas". So with that in mind customers and visitors are encouraged to adhere to very simple processes put in place, such as recycling their waste. And our in-house café and shop allow us promote our ideals, from sourcing organic clothing to growing organic food. By communicating to customers what we are doing, and why, we hope in a small way to influence them to make informed choices in their own lives.

Developing Sustainable Solutions

Sustainability is about making the right decisions for the long term, both for the business, our customers and the environment. This can be overwhelming for anyone starting on this journey, so we started small and simple: buying milk in recyclable glass bottles; separate bins for different waste streams; we stopped selling bottled water and instead fitted water fountains. Since these small beginnings we have changed most of our in-house processes and systems and are now concentrating on the bigger project of transforming the fabric of the Castle into an energy efficient building using sustainable building practices and materials and testing out some of the newest technologies around.

Waste Management

We've challenged the "throw-away" culture by adopting a holistic approach and educating all staff and visitors on waste management. Since we began we have reduced the size of our landfill bin collections by 78%.

- All staff receive training on waste management and our Environmental Policy is incorporated into every employee's terms of work.
- Our procurement policy applies to *all* staff and *every* purchase.
- Customers and staff are encouraged to stream waste through waste stations around the centre (including battery recycling).
- Encourage customers to deposit their food waste in our compost bins if they have no home collection.

- Development of our permaculture garden means we don't buy pre-packaged food; dried goods are bought in bulk and we produce garden herbs/teas reducing use of packaged herbs/teas.
- We give away old climbing holds to customers for home use.
- Our development works produce offcuts of wood – these have been made into garden tables and benches.
- Retired ropes are used for garden trellising or donated to local artists.
- Compost production is now at 3 tonnes a year (2013). Had we put this kitchen waste to landfill we would have produced 1.43 tonnes CO_2e (compared to just 15 kg by composting).
- Some food waste feeds our two small wormeries. Wormeries efficiently turn food waste into a nutrient-rich liquid fertilizer.

Sustainable food

One of the biggest areas of change was the development of the green space that surrounds the climbing centre into a permaculture growing site. Work began in earnest in 2009 and five years later the garden is a thriving space which not only provides organic produce for our own café throughout most of the year, but also grows salad and veg for Growing Communities and provides plots for staff and the local community to grow their own food.

We have replaced all the pre-made food we bought in with homemade versions. The kitchen produces hot meals, soups, cakes, tray bakes, jams and pickles, utilizing all the salad, vegetable and fruits that we grow here on site. 2012 was the first year we began weighing and recording food harvested, with 428.33 kilos supplied to the café.

We have a large number of herb beds so we can offer fresh herbal teas to customers throughout the summer months. A drying room was built in 2011 to enable us to dry a huge amount of herbs and flowers to sell in tea blends throughout the winter months. See www.castle-climbing.co.uk/Direct-from-garden-to-mug for more information about the 40+ varieties of herbs growing in our garden and how they're processed.

In 2013 we added a cob oven and roundhouse to the garden, built by staff and volunteers, providing the Castle community with a natural space to get together, make pizzas and bake bread or just enjoy the peace and quiet.

Resource conservation

Water

In 2012 we installed eleven 1,000 litre tanks for rainwater harvesting. Five of these now water the forest garden and herb beds via porous pipes whilst another six feed into garden taps. An additional 4,000 litres of historical tanks have also been put to use and water other areas and fill the pond in times of drought.

In 2011 we constructed a swale in the garden and began directing water from the men's showers and sinks into the hillside as a natural irrigating system for the area. Ecover shower products are provided by the centre, encouraging customers to use eco-friendly products.

From making these improvements alone we have already seen a 14% decrease in mains water usage (2012 figures).

Work on the installation of composting toilets, to replace our current ones is planned to start in 2014 and once completed (in 2015) we will be as close to water neutral as we can be.

Electricity

All of our new building developments have LED lighting installed, with daylight and movement sensors as standard. Our new basement-level climbing walls (built in 2014) have low-energy daylight tubes fitted.

In 2013 we replaced some of the centre's matting under the climbing walls. This new matting is bright yellow, and coupled with the light-coloured walls, helps to reflect as much natural daylight as possible into the centre.

In the next big phase of our developments we will replace the current leaking roof with a super-insulated one with auto-actuating sky lights for natural ventilation and solar PV panels fitted for electricity generation. We intend to generate our own electricity on site and once the panels are fitted we should be able to produce in the region of 45,000 kWh/yr of electricity.

Gas

The planned new roof, the installation of air source heat pumps and a new revolving front entrance door will hopefully further reduce the need for gas heating. We have already started by insulating the office and installing under-floor heating which will be used with an air source heat pump once installed.

In 2013 we moved to Ecotricity for our gas and electricity supply. We want to support Ecotricity's plans to develop green gas mills in the UK as an alternative to continuing to rely on fossil fuels.

Experiences

As previously mentioned, the hardest challenge has been making that cultural shift: for example, persuading both customers and staff to adhere to waste management strategy. It *has* been a success and we *have* reduced our waste output, but even getting people to do something as simple as put rubbish in the right bins isn't easy. We have found it hard to keep that momentum going and keep both staff and customers enthused without sounding like a whinging parent. We also have to be very careful not to "lecture" our customers and risk alienating them. After all, they are our bread and butter and they visit the centre to climb in a relaxed, friendly atmosphere, not to be lectured on saving the planet.

On the other side of the same coin, when it comes to recruiting new staff, we are attracting applicants who are not just interested in the climbing aspect, but also those who have a keen interest in conservation. In turn they bring their own expertise (such as vegan cooking or how to build a solar dryer) and re-enthuse the staff with new ideas and new experiences.

We have learned a lot through our mistakes and successes. Sustainability within the business sector is a relatively new idea and is constantly changing and moving forward. We have learned that it takes a lot of time and human resources to keep pace with all the new ideas and technologies. As we have no one person dedicated to keeping up-to-date with new developments, deciding on a new lighting system or what supplier to use for our cleaning products takes a lot of research, time that we can't always afford whilst trying to run a large, busy climbing wall.

We knew from the beginning that the objectives we had set out for ourselves would not always be easy, and not always financially rewarding. We learned to take the quick wins and be happy– such as implementing the simple things like changing our electricity supplier to one with green credentials. Do the simple (and the free) things first as there are lots of resources out there to help and guide you. You don't have to reinvent the wheel every time.

The permaculture garden is our biggest success in terms of being able to show people what being sustainable can mean. Customers, visitors and staff can see the food growing in our garden and then wander upstairs to our café and eat the produce. It's great that we can so easily see a reduction in our carbon footprint due to cutting out a fair number of food miles and packaging waste, plus being able to convert our waste food into compost, thus creating a closed-loop system. However, much more important to us has been the cultural and community engagement. The garden is hugely inspiring to all who visit, for staff, customers and volunteers who work in the garden and for school and community groups who use it as a teaching tool.

The Future

We understand that we are in charge of an important piece of London's industrial heritage and we intend, throughout the design process, to retain and display as many of the historical features as we can whilst balancing our mission to become environmentally sustainable and to "green" this leaky old Victorian building.

In the next few years we plan to redevelop both sets of changing rooms, redesigning the showers to be more energy-efficient and install composting toilets. Our reception area is draughty and very cold in winter, so our architects are working on a new layout which will create a more insulated working area that doesn't cost the earth to heat and will improve the working conditions for our reception staff too. The pump rooms and a further two wells from the original pumping station will be developed into more climbing and training rooms, using sustainable materials and building techniques, in line with what we have already built.

The most expensive and biggest jobs will be to re-do the whole roof and install solar panels. All of these further developments of the Castle are viewed as long-term projects which we will be undertaking over a number of years to keep the project as economically sustainable as possible.

Authors

Efua Uiterwijk (Centre Manager) has worked for the Castle for seven years and been instrumental in the change of this small business from a straightforward leisure enterprise into a fully sustainable business, leaving no area of operations unexamined. Efua has given talks on sustainable business practices and is always willing to share ideas and give advice to other organizations as part of the goal to communicate awareness of sustainability across all sectors.

Efua@castle-climbing.co.uk   020 8211 1072

Claire Lee (Marketing & Events Coordinator) has worked for the Castle for four years and is responsible for the organization's environmental reporting as well as implementing measures across the business. With over 10 years' experience in marketing and events, Claire's work in promoting the Castle's drive for sustainability, both internally and externally, has been vital. We are proud to support many local projects through events and workshops and Claire is always keen to hear from anyone with new ideas to join the Castle's ever expanding "green" network.

Claire@castle-climbing.co.uk   020 8211 1075

United House, NHP Leisure Developments and Mitsubishi Electric (joint award)

www.unitedhouse.net

Award: Sustainable Building

The Mission

United House is a leading housing specialist offering innovative solutions across London and the south as a contractor and regeneration partner. The group undertakes projects that span social housing new build, refurbishment, urban regeneration, mixed-use, Public Private Partnerships and private residential schemes. Sustainability is at the heart of United House's work, which is continually measured through a series of short and long-term objectives as part of the company's commitment to Corporate Social Responsibility.

The company is a pioneer of low-carbon retrofit and has a reputation for taking a positive stance on sustainable construction and, as such, was the ideal partner to help realize Mike Spenser-Morris, Managing Director of

NHP Leisure Developments, vision for a zero-carbon sustainable mixed-use development for Kingston Heights in Kingston town centre, Surrey. The development was to become the UK's first residential scheme to receive all of its heating, hot water and cooling requirements from solar energy naturally stored in the River Thames.

Approximately 50% of carbon emissions in the UK arise from the production of thermal energy. Whereas a great deal of attention has been paid to the production of green electricity, relatively little has been paid to the green production of heat. Mike Spenser-Morris's aim at Kingston was to demonstrate that it is possible to economically produce the 2.3 megawatts of thermal energy required by the development without burning any gas or wood pellets, and in doing so totally eradicate on-site carbon emissions, whilst at the same time increasing energy efficiency by at least 500% to 1,000% when compared to a combustion-based district heating system. For with global CO_2 emissions now at an all-time high, and demand for the planet's energy resources increasing all the time, it is fundamental that we change the way in which we think about the provision of thermal energy for new homes, and on a larger scale, entire cities.

The Challenge

Kingston Heights is a large-scale £70m mixed-use development located 200 metres from the River Thames. The scheme, built by United House on behalf of NHP Leisure Developments, comprises 137 residential apartments (81 private and 56 affordable homes – managed by Affinity

Sutton) and a 142-bedroom four-star hotel and conference centre.

From the outset, Mike Spenser-Morris had sought to equip Kingston Heights with a thermal energy system that would utilize natural resources to their maximum potential to provide all of the necessary heating, hot water and cooling requirements for the scheme. He wanted to demonstrate that, with the right determination and approach, a district heating system served by an Open Water Heat Pump is a far superior alternative to conventional installations.

However, given that this was a UK first, Mike was initially faced with the problem of providing proof to his own team that that the system would actually work. It took a great deal of effort to identify, and then, with Mitsubishi Electric's assistance, visit a similar example in Osaka, Japan before the proposal finally found acceptance. It was then necessary to deal with the red tape – local authority approvals, Environment Agency licences, etc. – within a very tight timeframe in order to bring the scheme to fruition.

Developing Sustainable Solutions

United House was duly appointed to construct the scheme, in light of the company's sustainability credentials and shared vision to deliver a landmark eco project that could pave the way for others to follow. However, the only way of resolving the "red tape" issues quickly led Mike to approach the MP for Kingston and Surbiton, Ed Davey, who had also just become the Secretary of State for Energy and Climate Change. Immediately recognizing the importance of the new system, he gave the Kingston installation his full support, and his assistance proved invaluable.

As a result, Kingston Heights is now a reality, and the first installation in the UK to utilize a system that recovers the solar energy stored naturally within the river water as the energy source to provide the thermal energy for the development. The scheme, which utilizes Mitsubishi Electric's advanced heat pump technology, produces zero on-site carbon emissions, in contrast to the estimated 500 tonnes of CO_2 that would otherwise be emitted by a combustion-based system.

The first step in the project was the encapsulation of a UKPN main grid substation that serves the Royal Borough of Kingston – and therefore had to remain fully operational at all times – around which the development was to be built. Another "first", this significant civil engineering project – a £20 million development in its own right – had never been done in the UK before. The substation was encased within a steel-lined concrete "box" 200 metres long, 38 metres wide and four storeys high. Above this, a podium deck was formed to create a foundation for the apartments using 59 pre-stressed concrete beams, each 38 metres long and weighing 80 tonnes.

Having completed work on the encapsulation, United House worked with NHP to install the Open Water district heating system. Inside a specially built plant room adjacent to the river, up to 150 litres of water per second is abstracted from the River Thames, passing through a state-of-the-art, two-stage filtration process that ensures no marine life or detritus can enter the system, before passing through high-efficiency heat exchangers that harvest its "low grade" heat. The water is then immediately returned to the river, unchanged in any way, and at a temperature no more than ±3°C from the ambient water temperature, resulting in no harm to the river's ecology.

The system works on the principle that two metres below the surface the water remains constant at around 8 to 10°C, making it a permanent, scalable source of renewable energy that is available 24/7/365, regardless of daylight, weather or air temperature.

The low grade heat thus transferred from the river to an internal "closed loop" water system is then circulated 200 metres to a plant room in the apartment building, from which it is distributed to one of six vertical risers serving the residential development, plus the hotel plant room. Thirty-nine Mitsubishi Electric heat pumps positioned locally to the flats they are serving in the risers boost the low grade 8–10°C temperature up to the 45°C needed for the apartments' underfloor heating and hot water requirements.

The system will also serve the hotel's hot water demands as well as the fan coil units' heating and cooling circuits. Heat rejected from the hotel's cooling cycle will be recycled into the closed-loop system to assist, in the first instance, with the provision of the hotel's own DHW requirements, and if that is fully satisfied, the heating and hot water requirements for the residential apartments.

100% of the electricity required to run the system comes from Ecotricity's wind turbines. As a result Kingston Heights has a Zero Carbon, 2.3 MW thermal energy system that will save over 500 tonnes of CO_2 that would otherwise have been dumped into the environment by an alternative combustion-based system each and every year.

Furthermore, the system has a Coefficient of Performance (CoP) of between 4 and 6+, making it one of the most energy-efficient schemes in the country. As a result of that energy efficiency, it is anticipated that residents will save approximately 16–20% on their annual heating bills when compared to an individual, fully maintained gas boiler – good news when governments around the world are keen to keep consumers' energy costs down.

Experiences

Ed Davey and his senior officials at the Department of Energy and Climate Change have warmly welcomed the installation at Kingston Heights, which they regard as an exemplar system for the rest of the UK.

A programme of work has been instigated within the Ministry that is aimed at encouraging and facilitating others around the country to adopt the system wherever large-scale development is taking place in reasonable proximity to an open body of water – be it a river, lake, waterway or the sea.

The first step of this process was to produce the first iteration of a National Water Source Heat Map (to be updated/expanded later in the year) that indicates where the largest concentrations of development are taking place that could optimize the use of the system, and therefore maximize the Carbon Reduction benefits.

The second step is to inform the various local and central government bodies and other agencies about the system in order to remove, in advance, the potential obstacles

– both related to principle and time – that existed at Kingston. This is a programme that is now underway.

Widely encouraged to make the extensive in-depth knowledge available to other projects, Mike Spenser-Morris has now established The Zero Carbon Partnership (www.ZeroCarbonPartnership.com) to offer comprehensive advice and assistance to anyone interested in adopting the technology.

From a sustainability point of view, the successes of Kingston Heights do not stop at the benefits provided by the revolutionary heating system. The entire construction process was undertaken with sustainability in mind and, as such, United House put into place rigorous procedures to ensure its carbon footprint was reduced during the build. Construction waste was reduced thanks to the use of off-site pre-fabrication of major construction components, pre-cast concrete beams and astute measuring of all material requirements, ensuring minimal wastage. All timber and steel waste was recycled and segregated. The project was certified by the Community Wood Recycling social enterprise as having diverted 70% tonnes of timber waste for re-use or recycling.

From a townscape and community perspective, an unsightly and noisy electricity substation site has been transformed into an architecturally magnificent development that has had a significant impact on the regeneration of this part of Kingston's town centre. Environmentally, the benefits are considerable, with a previously barren site now providing the residents with over half an acre of beautifully landscaped communal roof gardens, plus significant areas of tree planting and soft landscaping around the development at ground level to complete the area's transformation.

The Future

Centralized district heating systems are attractive – they can produce large amounts of thermal energy for large-scale development more efficiently than the traditional individual gas boiler. But having to burn large quantities of fossil base material, whether gas, wood, oil or coal, to produce large quantities of heat today seems antiquated.

The act of burning produces carbon emissions, and to burn a lot of anything produces a lot of carbon emissions. It is also not energy-efficient to circulate large quantities of hot water over long distances, with the inevitable heat losses along the way. A CoP of 0.6 to 0.8 is normal, whereas the Open Water Heat Pump system can produce CoPs of 4 to 6+.

Installation is straightforward. Unlike a combustion boiler-based system which requires, expensive insulation, the below ground circulation pipework is uninsulated – the ground itself providing the insulation for the low-grade temperature of the closed-loop system. And maintenance of a system with few moving parts and nothing that gets hot is easier and more economical.

The most vital thing that now needs to be achieved is to publicize and spread the word about the Open Water Heat Pump system and its wide-ranging benefits. For once potential adopters become aware of the system, how it works and the advantages of using it, it is likely to soon become the automatic thermal installation of choice – to the benefit of the planet.

Contact Details

www.unitedhouse.net/contact-us   0132 266 5522

Images

1. Kingston Grid site before construction

2. Kingston Heights CGI: the vision

3. Massive beams are delivered to site

4. Beams craned into position

5. Fully encapsulated substation

6. The new pump house

7. Thames Venturer

8. Lowering the filtration into the Thames

9. The heat exchangers

10. 200 m of pipe installation carry the water to the scheme

11. Flow and return pipework up to the fifth-floor plant room

12. Scheme pump switch-on, October 2013

13. The control panel

14. Controlling the river water

15. Completed scheme (1)

16. Completed scheme (2)

17. Completed scheme (3)

104 SUSTAINABLE CITIES

UNITED HOUSE, NHP LEISURE DEVELOPMENTS AND MITSUBISHI ELECTRIC 105

106 SUSTAINABLE CITIES

108 SUSTAINABLE CITIES

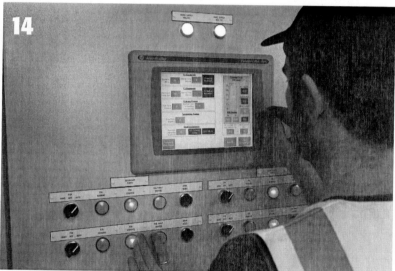

UNITED HOUSE, NHP LEISURE DEVELOPMENTS AND MITSUBISHI ELECTRIC 111

WestTrans Partnership

www.westtrans.org

Award: Sustainable Travel and Transport

The Mission

WestTrans is a partnership of the six West London boroughs of Ealing, Brent, Hammersmith & Fulham, Harrow, Hillingdon and Hounslow. Led by Ealing Council, it works with Transport for London and other regional stakeholders to identify, develop and implement strategic transport projects for the benefit of the sub-region. Alongside the highly successful transitional process of the Partnership Review, recent activity has seen a strong focus on strategic Travel Planning programmes.

The Challenge

Between secondary school and employment there is a lack of guidance in promoting sustainable modes of travel to those enrolled in higher and further education institutions. However, it is at this time that individuals start to form travel habits and behaviours that they will adopt when starting full-time employment.

WestTrans recognized this gap and undertook a Green Travel Programme of educational events and engagement.

Developing Sustainable Solutions

HE/FE Green Travel Days were originally organized to promote sustainable travel through exhibitions in the Students Union/s. WestTrans delivered a pilot project in 2010 focusing on two large universities in the sub-region (Brunel University and University of West London). Based on the success of the pilot, we developed a more comprehensive programme attempting to engage with all the HE/FE sites in the sub-region.

The programme includes a range of complementary activities and events that promote green travel. Building on the Travel Plan and Delivery Strategy, the programme targets higher and further education students and staff and can potentially include a Green Travel Exhibition Day, Social Engagement events, charity events and/or led cycle/walks. This is done through an interactive activity as well as raising the awareness of smarter travel choices.

WestTrans commissioned a specialist consultancy to provide the hands-on support for these events. In 2012/13 over the course of supporting the coordination of these events, the following outcomes were quantified.

- 10 days of events scheduled (4 above the original target)
- 20 sustainable transport exhibitors booked

- Reach of approximately 81,000
- Over 2,500 recorded event attendees
- Over 400 individuals taking part in the smarter driving or cycle simulators
- Revised "Green Travel Day" pack produced
- Engaged with 7 out of 10 institutions in the sub-region (*University of Brunel, University of West London, Westminster University, Harrow College, Stanmore College, West Thames College and Uxbridge College*)
- Key contacts (active travel champions) established at all the sites

The support provided, assisted HE organizations to deliver smarter travel events and engagement activities for students and staff. This included guidance in setting up the event, and a smarter travel "event pack" enabling the HE organization to run its own events in the future.

WestTrans has developed a HE/FE Event Day toolkit to share the lessons learned to other institutions that would like to replicate this programme. The purpose of this toolkit is to:

- Provide sufficient information to enable institutions to deliver a programme of promoting Green Travel.
- Encourage staff and students to take responsibility for travel issues.
- Provide attractive, user friendly downloadable materials to assist institutions.
- Build upon the institution's travel plan to actively encourage a shift from car to more sustainable,

healthy modes of travel (e.g. walking, cycling and public transport).
- Highlight examples of WestTrans pilot studies of good practice locally.
- Clearly reference other appropriate sources of travel plan guidance and assistance.

Experiences

As students are always travelling to and from their establishments, educating them about the environment is definitely a quick win. Through raising awareness about the benefits of smarter travel choices – improving health, saving money, reducing emissions and improving air quality – we equip this demographic to make a more informed choice of how their travel behaviour effects the world around them.

The Green Travel days contribute to the overall wellbeing of the region as it delivers on some key issues that the boroughs are working on. These include contributing to alleviating poor air quality through change in travel mode, an increase in physical activity to help deliver some public health objectives and overall a greater awareness and connection with how the student's travel behaviours affect the world around them.

> **"It is great to see students involved with something that has a great deal of competition but also has the influence and scope to make a change on our long-term future."**
> James Ward, Vice President Community Welfare, Union of Brunel Students

> "This is the first event of its type Harrow College have run and we did really enjoy it. It was a very popular event – more popular than we expected and was attended by over 250 students who enjoyed the interactive nature of the event. From those who completed the quiz 83% said they enjoyed the day and 65% said they would consider cycling to College in the future. We will definitely run an event again in the future."
> Claire Savaryn, Estates & Environment Coordinator, Harrow College

With 2013 being hailed as the "Year of Air" we built on our programme by incorporating a greater emphasis on air quality. This is innovative and demonstrates leadership in the field as there isn't currently a similar programme looking at how HE/FE students and staff's travel impacts on air quality and how greater awareness around this and encouragement of behaviour change can be elicited.

We have tailored the programme to include activity to support the Mayor's Air Quality Strategy including: the promotion of low-emission vehicles (such as electric cars) and eco-driving. WestTrans have been successful in being awarded some funding through the Mayor Air Quality Fund programme and will ensure that each site can run two activities one of which will be focussed on Air Quality.

Through previous years we have learned that the competitive side helps to engage students who don't usually participate with these sorts of projects. This means offering targeted simulators for the events planned this year such as:

- ECO Drive Simulator
- The Walkit "low pollution" urban walking route planner
- NipNip leasing of electric bikes for business

- E-Car: The Electric Vehicle Car Club
- Blue Door Bicycles or E-Bikes Direct London

WestTrans is confident that the HE/FE sites will continue to follow our leadership in this area as demonstrated by an increase in participation year on year.

When asked if they would be willing to run a Green Travel day again and why, the overwhelming response was positive with reasons including:

- "Yes I'd be keen to run another sustainable transport day, possibly with more support for the simulators and to provide people with further information and context. I would be keen to have something similar take place in the autumn to encourage new students" (University of West London).
- "Yes we would be very pleased to run a sustainable transport day again and make it an annual event as it supports our sustainable development policy and encourages students to engage in healthy activity and cut their carbon emissions" (Harrow College).

The HE/FE sites are showing leadership by taking part and making it a regular fixture in their event calendars. This way they are able to capture a new audience when fresher's and a new intake of students come in. These are the key times to try and influence a mode shift, when people are making some type of life change (new job, new school, new home, etc.).

The Future

The programme is now in its third year of operation with engagement and participation growing annually. The initial pilot year saw just two HE/FE sites taking part in the Green event day; the following year had seven organizations taking part.

WestTrans is regarded as a beacon of excellence in the delivery of new and innovative behaviour change initiatives. This is evidenced by a series of knowledge sharing events with practitioners from across the globe. We facilitate visits for representatives of various transport authorities. In 2012/13 we had visits from the Abu Dhabi Department of Transport (DoT) and Singapore's Land Transport Authority (LTA) to share best practice increase awareness of the tools that can be employed to facilitate travel behaviour change.

We also work hard to promote our activities and those of our partners through key marketing and promotional activities during the year which include:

- Bi-monthly partnership meetings
- Re-design of the WestTrans website
- Quarterly e-newsletters
- Chairing of various networks across the sub-region
- Facilitating visits from practitioners across the globe

The website is a key hub for our stakeholders; providing details of projects, past and present as well as details of events, partnership meetings and publications.

WestTrans is very proactive in developing case studies for the projects and initiatives that we deliver. This is to enable other businesses, local authorities or networks interested in travel demand management and behaviour change to replicate our work. We have an open approach to knowledge sharing, and with the current climates of tighter budgets and scrutiny, we provide toolkits and templates of key projects (HE/FE Green days toolkit, Residential travel planning toolkit, hotel journey planner) free to use.

WestTrans has a Challenge Fund which supports the growth of local provision for Travel Planning across the region. Challenge Fund bids are match funded by the organization applying. In the past year thousands of pounds of match funding has been awarded, including just over £3,000 to support NHS sites in the region with Legible London style "active travel maps" for use during the Olympics.

Author

Tim Forrester (WestTrans Manager) is a highly experienced transport planning professional and project manager who has worked in west London for the past ten years on a wide range of strategic transport and behaviour change programmes. He has worked across the six west London boroughs of Ealing, Brent, Hammersmith & Fulham, Harrow, Hillingdon and Hounslow to deliver mutually beneficial projects, cost savings and joined up policy for the wider benefit of the region.

ForresterT@ealing.gov.uk